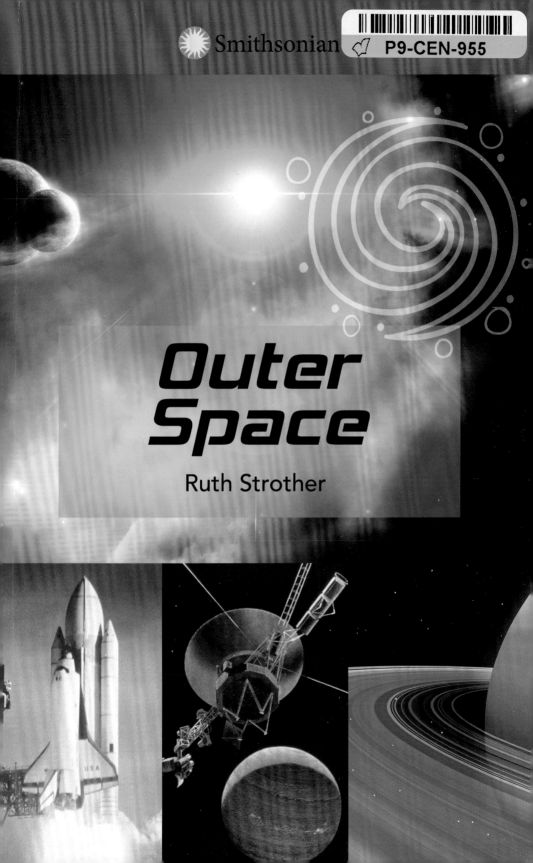

Outer Space

Ruth Strother

Contents

Outer space is huge.
The universe contains everything
we can see.
No one knows where it ends.
Stars, planets, and moons can be
found in outer space.

Stars

Stars are bright balls of burning gas.
Stars can burn for billions of years.
The Sun is a star.
It is the closest star to Earth.

People draw pretend lines between some stars.
The lines form shapes.
The shapes look like people and animals.
These shapes are called **constellations**.

The Solar System

The Sun is the only star in our solar system. The Sun is the center of our solar system. The word *solar* means "of the Sun."

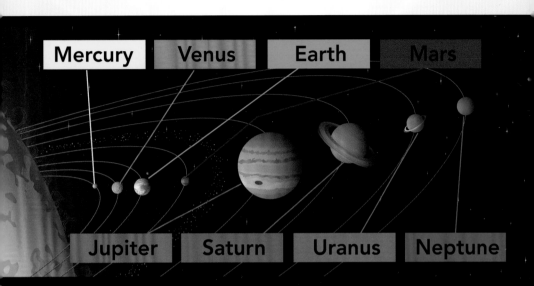

Mercury Venus Earth Mars

Jupiter Saturn Uranus Neptune

The Sun's **gravity** pulls planets into a path. The path leads planets around the Sun.

We live on the planet Earth.
Earth is part of the solar system.

Planets

Planets are objects in space.
Planets must follow a path around
a star.
Our solar system has eight planets.

Each planet is round.
Each planet follows a path around
the Sun.
This path is called an **orbit**.
And each planet is the only big
object in its orbit.

Inner Planets

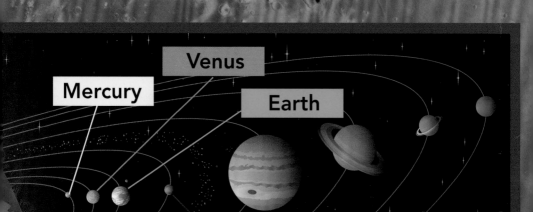

Mercury
Venus
Earth
Mars

Four planets are closer to the Sun.
They are Mercury, Venus, Earth, and Mars.
They are the inner planets.

Inner planets are small, solid, and rocky.

Mercury is the smallest planet in the solar system.

Venus is the brightest planet seen from Earth.

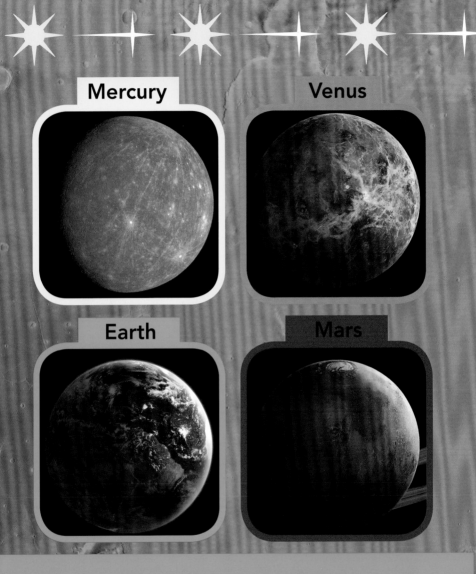

Mercury

Venus

Earth

Mars

Earth is the only planet with liquid water on its surface.

Mars has the tallest mountain in the solar system.

The gas planets are Jupiter, Saturn, Uranus, and Neptune. They are not solid. They are gassy, almost like clouds. Spaceships can't land on them.

Jupiter is the biggest planet in the solar system.

Saturn has rings made of ice, dust, and rocks.

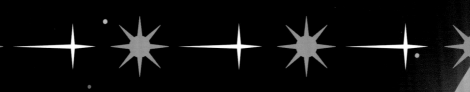

Uranus is the coldest planet in the solar system.

Neptune is the windiest planet in the solar system.

Jupiter

Saturn

Uranus

Neptune

Moons

Moons are space objects.
Moons orbit a planet.
The planet's gravity keeps a moon on its path.

Some planets have many moons.
Some planets have no moon at all.

Earth has one moon.

Jupiter has more moons than any other planet.
Jupiter has sixty-seven moons!

Comets

Comets are dust and rocks trapped in ice.
Comets orbit the Sun.
Comets have a tail.
The tail points away from the Sun.

Comets melt a little when they get close to the Sun.
Some comets crash into a planet or a moon.
These comets leave big holes called **craters**.

Asteroids are made of rocks.
Asteroids orbit the Sun, just like planets do.
But asteroids are too small to be planets.
Most asteroids are found between Mars and Jupiter.

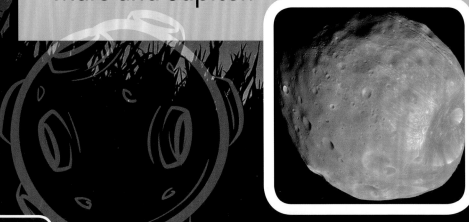

Meteoroids are made of rocks and metals.
Meteoroids are smaller than asteroids.
But meteoroids orbit the Sun too.
Sometimes asteroids and meteoroids fall to Earth.

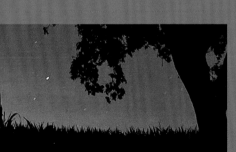

Meteors, Meteorites, and Shooting Stars

Meteors are meteoroids that get close to Earth.
Meteors burn when they get close to Earth.
Meteors look like flashes of light.
We call them shooting stars!

Sometimes meteors don't burn up. Sometimes meteors land on Earth. Then they are called meteorites.

Galaxies are made of dust, gas, and billions of stars.
Billions of galaxies spin in outer space.
Earth and our solar system are part of a galaxy.

Our galaxy has hundreds of billions of stars!
From Earth, the stars look like a pathway of milk.
Our galaxy is called the Milky Way.

Astronauts

Astronauts travel to outer space. Some astronauts learn how to fly a spaceship.

Astronauts learn how to move in a spacesuit.
Some astronauts learn how to study outer space.

astronauts

American astronauts train at NASA.
But astronauts come from other
countries too.

Astronauts are called cosmonauts
in Russia.
The first person in space
was a cosmonaut.

cosmonaut

Spaceships and Space Stations

The first spaceship was the size of a soccer ball.

Now spaceships are big. Spaceships carry astronauts into outer space.

Some astronauts live and work in space.

Their job is to study outer space. They stay in outer space for many months.

These astronauts live and work in space stations.

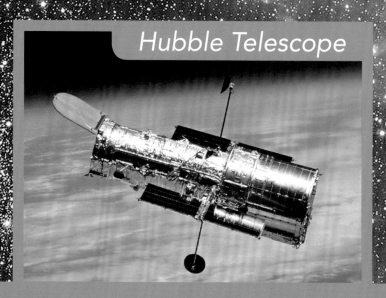

Hubble Telescope

We can't get to many parts of outer
space.
So we send up robots and **telescopes**.
They explore space for us.
They send us new facts.

Mars Rover

We have a lot of outer space to explore.
Maybe someday you will be an astronaut.
Maybe you will work in a space station.
Maybe you will explore a new planet!

Outer Space QUIZ

1. How long can stars burn?
   a) Thousands of years
   b) Hundreds of years
   c) Billions of years

2. What does the word "solar" mean?
   a) "of outer space"
   b) "of the Sun"
   c) "of a star"

3. How many planets are in our solar system?
   a) Eight
   b) Five
   c) Nine

4. Which is the smallest planet in our solar system?
   a) Earth
   b) Jupiter
   c) Mercury

5. Which is the biggest planet in our solar system?
   a) Jupiter
   b) Saturn
   c) Mars

6. What is our galaxy called?
   a) A constellation
   b) The solar system
   c) The Milky Way

GLOSSARY

constellations: groups of stars that form shapes

craters: scooped-out areas made by space objects hitting a planet or moon

gravity: a force that pulls one object to another

orbit: the path one object takes around another object

telescope: a tool that makes distant objects look closer and bigger

Stars

Planets

Moons

Io Europa Ganymede Callisto

Galaxies

Meteors

Solar System

Planets are round objects in space that circle a star.

Stars are hot, bright balls of burning gas.

Galaxies are made of dust, gas, and billions of stars.

Moons are round objects in space that circle a planet.

Our solar system is the Sun and all the planets that circle it.

Meteors look like flashes of light that we call shooting stars.